Two

Tragedies

in 429

Breaths

Two

Tragedies

in 429

Breaths

SUSAN PADDON

BRICK BOOKS

BRICK BOOKS · 431 BOLER ROAD, BOX 20081
LONDON, ONTARIO N6K 4G6 · WWW.BRICKBOOKS.CA

Cover image, design and layout by Cheryl Dipede.
This book is set in Arno Pro, designed by Robert Slimbach
and first issued by Adobe in 2007.

The author photo was taken by Matthew Parsons.

Library and Archives Canada Cataloguing in Publication

Paddon, Susan, 1978-, author
           Two tragedies in 429 breaths / Susan Paddon.
Poems.
ISBN 978-1-926829-94-4 (pbk.)
           I. Title.
PS8631.A275T86 2014   C811'.6   C2014-903872-0

We acknowledge the Canada Council for the Arts, and the Ontario
Arts Council for their support of our publishing program.

Canada Council   Conseil des Arts
for the Arts   du Canada

ONTARIO ARTS COUNCIL
CONSEIL DES ARTS DE L'ONTARIO

In Loving Memory of

Barbara Gail Anderson Paddon
January 31, 1941 – August 13, 2008

For Pamela Joan and Russell Dean

CONTENTS

JUNE

JULY

AFTER

"Why are the songs so short?" a bird once asked.
"Is it because thou art short of breath?"
—A. Daudet, from *The Personal Papers of Anton Chekhov*

There are moments worth repeating.

The tenant of regret is never the one we expect.

I am going to tell you everything.

APRIL

(red ink on Loblaw's receipt)

Lately I find myself whispering to Maria
Chekhova in my head.

             Oh, sweet Masha, I say.

       I have come home to care for my mother.

Place on a Lake

"But I am drawn here to this lake like a seagull." (*The Seagull,* Anton Chekhov)

My mother lives in a house on a lake that freezes
in a thousand meringues every winter,
just beyond the shore. She does not live

alone. My father is with her. Together
they weave a happy front, eat McDonald's
on Mondays and pretend everything

will be okay. Life is a list they're getting
through. My father's roots are in this place

on the lake, though it is not what it once was
when the ferry still came from Cleveland, when
Lombardo played the bandstand, before

the factories and smokestacks that won't let my mother forget
this is not her home. She grew up beside an ocean,
with real orange trees in the front yard. Now

she dreams of those trees, you can see it in the way
she closes her curtains, lies awake at night

reliving conversations from bygone decades,
the sounds of misplaced emphases, the offences she may have caused,
help me think of something nice, she whispers to my father
to quiet the voices that keep repeating in the cold sheets.

CHIRRUP, CHIRRUP

There is a dog disturbing
a magnificent brown finch in the magnolia.
Bromide! I call. Even in my dreams
there is Anton Chekhov. The steppe
outside my window

cold as all hell.

In this dream the dog doesn't answer, but a stirring inside
my mother's house reminds me
I've been far away and must get back.

It is my mother who is closer to Chekhov. The wings inside her
changing like a peppered moth.

I am more Masha. The sister

who keeps secret watch,
notes blood on pillowcases.
I've read every cough he ever wrote, only
in my dreams they always seem to get better.

There's this recurring vision of a boy
who jumps foxholes on the steppe, who walks—
coat open— in the rain.

This House

a stage, set by my mother, object
by object, when she first got sick.
No two props more than three steps apart,
the distance she can travel now
without a pause. I am her leading stagehand,

Danchenko: driver, bodyguard. Like the old woman
at the Chekhov House Museum in Yalta
who keeps the books, looks after the upkeep and
collects tickets at the door.

A little boy runs through the garden in Yalta
while the old woman isn't looking,
eats the first raspberry off the bush.
With a pocket knife on his key ring, his father
cuts a small piece of the linoleum
from the front entrance of the writer's house.
Takes it back to Pennsylvania
for almost no reason at all.

Unsent Letter 1

To:
9 Cité Jandelle
Paris, 75019

Dearest J.,

You said you knew I was leaving even before the call came. You were the one who loved Chekhov first. His face tacked to your side of the room. His eyes between bars of light when the morning sun came in.

By day, you read obituaries for auction houses, prepared condolence cards for the inheritors of fine-coloured glass lamps and walnut tallboys. By night, you ate jars of white asparagus and palm hearts with chopsticks, immersed yourself in his books. You too would suck the poison from my wounds, you said— "The Grasshopper" butterflied across your lap—if that was all I required.

The day I left Paris, I cried all the way to the Gare du Nord, and not just because of my mother. You said you had the weight of lead in your guts. Until then, we'd agreed we both loved stations.

I promised you a lot of things I knew would be impossible once I was gone, and you defiantly promised nothing. You walked alongside the train as it pulled away. I watched you as you smoothed your hair. There was melancholy in the spring air. And in the darkening sky. And in the train car.

Breakfast

Now I read Chekhov's notebooks
and study his letters. I take them with me
to my oatmeal and toast. It's his inabilities
that interest me most. The number of steps
he couldn't take. The drink he couldn't have.
How he fell onstage, head thrown back
like a doll, when they made him take a bow.

In the next bedroom, the humidifier rattles.
The air filter hums. The walls reek of mould spray,
but there is no mould, never was. My mother
labours over each breath as she sleeps. We
don't know what is consuming her
and no one can help us.

When I was a child and lay next to her,
I synchronized my breath with hers.
I pretended I could climb in and out
of her belly like a kangaroo.

When Chekhov was too sick to leave his bed,
he counted knots in the wood paneling,
tied his thoughts up like bound letters, filed them
against the back surface of his mind. Maria always
warmed his pyjamas and kept the cupboards clean.
Fed the cranes in the yard.

There is Sun in the Garden

We will go to the flower market
after all. It's good for her to get out.

My father comes into the kitchen
with a milky green tea and a dark stain
on his company shirt. He took

early retirement from the telephone company
more than a decade ago. "I think I'll poach myself
an egg," he mumbles. He's quietly working

on his independence. We know
what time it is by the neighbouring school bell.
An electric zap, like a lab rat running

the wrong direction in an undersized maze.
A quarter to nine. It jolts us a dozen times
each day. Before the end of first period,

my mother manages to will herself
from the kitchen chair to the door,
out along the uneven cement path

to the car, with only the aid of a walker. Her breath
rattles, lungs an empty cage. I trail behind
with oxygen tanks. She gets half her body

draped over the passenger seat of the car,
her legs splayed out the door. Then the left,
then the right. *I did it,* she says.

Faith

"You don't believe in it, but I do. Somebody in Dostoevsky or Voltaire said that if there had not been a God men would have invented him." ("Ward No. 6," Anton Chekhov)

All I have of faith are memories from childhood. God smelled of mothballs, of fresh snow evaporating on the fur coats that hung in the long church corridor; he smelled of Oscar de la Renta by the room where we ate maple cookies and sometimes drank carton lemonade out of Styrofoam cups. Faith was something you could taste at the back of your throat, like metallic blood in the dentist's chair.

I remember my mother, her eyes tightly closed on the icy mountain road, her jaw clenched when my sister and I threw punches, her swollen cheeks when my father got sick and her brother died, the way she wrung her hands when I didn't come home when I said I would.

Easter Day

Church bells and distant canticles
called him to the street. He could walk
through everything, like the alleys

of Petersburg. He was ill-dressed
because the show wasn't going
his way. Maria's ivory cross
no longer around

his neck. She was always the first
to search, to drop everything, refuse
sleep until he came back home. The others

thought they knew better. Left him to wallow
in success for a while. But they'd turn
to her first. *We need a Chekhov play! A sister*

can work magic on a stubborn man—
he'll do anything for you, Maria!
Convoys of searching prayers

were sent off on his behalf,
knees to the floor next to her bed. He never
stopped counting on this. And

he was good to her, his sister. Save
that July when he couldn't manage a syllable
to put her mind at ease. Still,

if she had been born the walker. Someone who could get away on foot.

Who loved to roam the empty streets at night.

WATCHING

"If you are not afraid of being stung by the nettles, come by the narrow footpath that leads to the lodge, and let us see what is going on inside." ("Ward No. 6,"
Anton Chekhov)

My mother's neighbour is watching us
from her back garden again. It's not her eyes I see,
but the shadow she casts through
the old vine-covered latticework
that must have taken such
small hands to make.

Leona's neck is craned
towards the row of speckled green-
on-green leaves that separates
her yard from ours.

I know what she looks like
standing there, not because I can see her,
but because I have seen her
so many times before.

No one visits her now. Not even her
grown-up children. She has to get a man in
to cut the lawn.

In her arms she holds the little cocker spaniel
who's almost nine. All of her love
goes into that hold, into the way one hand
meets the other under his
spotted pink belly.

We have grown silent
on our side of the property line.
Leona listens to our silence
carefully, not to let us know
she is listening.

Something is not right, she thinks.
Perhaps it's her duty to keep an eye on us.
Keep tabs on who goes in and
out of this house. You never know
when you might be of use.

I go now to the hedge
where our gardens meet
to see if I can't say hello.
But her shadow has vanished.

I'd forgotten the small purple flowers,
still nameless in my memory,
that flourish here
in the shade.

MAY

"When I dream I am haunted by phantoms. People come to me, I hear voices and music, and I fancy I am walking through woods or by the seashore, and I long so passionately for movement, for interests ... Come, tell me, what news is there?" asked Ivan Dmitritch; "what's happening?" ("Ward No. 6," Anton Chekhov)

(black ink on Coca-Cola carton)

I am convinced I hear Maria moving in the night.

She slips around the house with stealthy footsteps. She listens
for breaths, counts them on a wooden abacus,
notes them in a book.

Masha, I call out,

Where have you been?

Yellow

wafts in from the garden.

"We're in for a hot one," my mother says, her hand pivoting
towards the large bay window. There are aspects
of her skin I'd not noticed before, edges
rough like chipped porcelain—dips and waves
of paper flesh. I can feel her

eyes somewhere around my mouth,
although I am trying to focus
on an article about babies reading
lips. Any moment she will begin

the daily recitation of what *we* need
to get done: windows, carpets. Yesterday

we acquired a shredder for the boxes
of papers under her bed. In the early

editions of Chekhov's letters, his editors removed
anything that might stain his image or the image
of Russia. Ellipses, like little brooks across the page,

stand in for vulgar language, deleterious remarks and
the references to masturbation he used. But as far
as I know, no one made confetti of his personal life.

If it were up to me, I'd prefer to talk today. To ask
my mother questions, finish half-told stories.

Who was Penny again? Why did you leave Fort Lauderdale?
Did Dad ever write you letters? Are they under your bed?

I wonder whether my parents know one another's bodies.
The depth of his belly button, her right breast from the left.
Have they had a last night? Do you do that
when someone is dying? I want to record

the way her cheekbones
rise up to show off the intricate mechanism
where elegance and functionality still meet, despite
the swelling from the steroids.

I have already imagined after.

How eventually it will be my cheekbones
and the rough edges of my skin
that will return her to me,
like everything else
she passes on.

CHEKHOV'S SISTER, 1873

Two legs deep in the water—
there was this girl, Maria,
beside her brother fishing. She—the sister—
held a blanket
so that he wouldn't drown.

Before drying him off, she checked
his scrawny body and big head
for leeches. He hardly noticed her
there among the brambles, the bracken.

They walked along the train tracks home, single file
together, as lovers do
in wasted moments.
Kicked up dust, both of them, deliberates.
She, there to keep him company,
not to tell the others
he needed her.

My Mother's Sister

sent a new tablecloth in the post
a week before Christmas every year until
she started forgetting that too. When she lived in New York,
she had our names put onto even our lunch bags:
Susan, Susan, Susan. I carried it under my arm
like a teddy bear.

With my mother's sister it happened suddenly
and then slowly, and my mother has spent
so much of her life afraid (no aluminum, no
aspartame) of losing something very different
from what she is going to lose.

I once heard about a woman
who wouldn't have anything to do with garlic.
It wasn't fair, the way it could look perfect
from the outside and yet,
if you got unlucky, under the skin
it could already have turned.

My Sister,

a ketchuped potato chip in her mouth, plunged in after the Cambodian
mother and her child, new to our mother's church, just before

they started going under. The girl's hair billowing like a manta ray
as she bobbed up and down. They explained after, they didn't know

the swimming pool got deep. Years later, when our grandmother
didn't answer, my sister kicked her door down, found her just in time,

one leg splayed like a wishbone on the floor. She rescued butterflies
from windshields, transported house mice to the woods. She never forgets

anniversaries, goes home for birthdays, knows the inches of our father's
collar, what Royal Doultons our mother still doesn't have. When she

has dinner parties for thirty people, it is a failure on her part if a guest
has to ask where the bathroom is or where to put his coat. Her cat is sick:

shits and pisses on the furniture that was new last year, so she feeds him
organic biscuits from the specialty shop. My sister is pregnant for the first

time. This is why, when she visits, it's my job to run interference. Tidy up,
hide the puffers, the oxygen store, make excuses for the wheelchair

down the hall. For my mother, there is no room for more worry, and a baby
trumps everything else.

MARIA, 1878

Because it was a summer of brothers. Because
Taganrog was a stinkpot in July. Because they were five
for the holidays with their parents gone
on a pilgrimage (Moscow,
holy relics, polytechnic exhibition,
rich cousins in Shuia).

But really because Maria
would remember the names of backstreet brothels,
the then-foreign stench of lust and sweat
on her brothers' coats, the stories
she could never
get clean.

Two Gardens

On their first date, Chekhov took Olga Knipper
to his home in Melikhovo. He showed her
his pond, his flowers and—her favourite—the kitchen garden.
The courgettes, the garlic, the sugar-snap peas.
They played patience while the sun drew lines
in the earth, the samovar whistled, and their cheeks
grew sore from constant grinning. In the evening, she chased him
around the edges of the property. When it got dark,
they went inside to make love.

It is May. My mother is watching me plant the flowers
we bought, instructing me geranium by geranium, purple
agapanthuses, recalling what it meant to be in love
in the springtime of her youth. Nils Bergman took her
to see *Lawrence of Arabia* in Nashville
on a rainy night. Her hair got soaked
as they came out of the late showing, but it didn't matter.
Nothing did, because there were still deserts between
there and now, and Nils Bergman
kissed her that night for the first and last time.

Peaches

"In the intervals they lie down, sleep, look out of the window, and walk from one corner to the other. And so every day." ("Ward No. 6," Anton Chekhov)

Something like light crawls over the tabletop. This morning
I am a baby in need of a hip. "How do you spell 'pappardelle?'

And 'nostalgia?'" my mother asks. She has been watching a chipmunk
and doing the crossword. In the derelict BBQ, my father

found the chipmunk's nest. It was a heap of weather-struck leaves
and pink insulation mined from under the house.

Now the little creature stands homeless
on the lip of the deck.

"It must have carried the fibreglass one piece at a time."
There is a pause. "Here, have a peach," she says.

Last night, I calculated that thirty minutes
is approximately 429 breaths for a healthy person.
Half of that for someone with a compromised
respiratory system. For my mother,

it is the time it takes
to put on a pair of shoes
or to eat a peach. Chekhov

periodically slept in his shirt and trousers
so in the morning he wouldn't
have to waste time.

There is something about the way
the chipmunk stares out
over the wooden precipice
that makes me worry. I imagine

she is probably pregnant
and now has no home,
and there is bound to be insulation
in her lungs.

"Peaches aren't what they used to be," my father
mumbles from the living-room couch.
And then it happens.

A wave comes up from under
me, and I distinctly feel that I am a vessel
full of loose water and blood. I exhale into the table,
my body folded against the pine slats,
and I find I am crying for the first time.

When it finally stops,
it's almost as though she feels sorry for me,
this chipmunk, who looks back
through the open window
as she scampers away,
a V in the clover and vetch.

Room 45, Hotel Dresden, Moscow

I like to imagine
peacock wallpaper and starched sheets. The bathroom
down the hall.

Before they married, it was their meeting place
each time he came to the city.

And if she got there first, straight from rehearsal, did she stand,
shoulders back, before the long dusty mirror to practise not being Arkadina
for a while? Her hair let loose at the temples
like a pair of ribbons. She rubbed rosewater
on her knees and feet.

On the way up, *two lemonades*, he might have told the bellboy, and
a kopeck not to return again that evening. Did he stop each time
on the landing to catch his breath,

hoping to hear a quarrel somewhere down the hall?
It was such a long journey from the South.

I know how she would have undressed him,
slowly at first (he wore so many layers). They climbed under the white
of the white sheets. Outside, the city fast asleep.

And how many times he must have almost whispered
with his nose pressed to the back of her head,

they had everything

if wanting was enough.

Unsent Letter 2

To:
9 Cité Jandelle
Paris, 75019

Dearest J.,

It feels like an eternity and yesterday since we saw one another. I picture you, cigarette in hand, on the balcony of our flat. Do you still wear that blue terrycloth robe outside?

Today is the Portes Ouvertes. On your way up the hill, you will pass three boulangeries with meringue in their windows, resist each time because there are milles feuilles on boulevard Simone Bolivar worth holding out for. The street cleaners will spray the sidewalks as you pass. When you arrive in Belleville, you will visit as many ateliers as the morning will allow. Your favourite remains the one that makes staircases. Treads, risers, balusters in heaps upon the floor. You'll wonder what might become of them—where those staircases will lead to once you've left. Later, you'll eat lamb couscous at the restaurant on rue Marie with everybody else.

It's Sunday. My father has taken my mother to church.

I wonder how you remember me. Do you think of me from time to time? I don't go anywhere now but to the shops and back.

NOTEBOOK

This is a trap. I know I'm being watched. It's the hidden
cameras in the kitchen of my childhood,
and I have just licked the serving bowl clean.

I open my notebook.

1. Penny was my mother's friend who disappeared
and for whom my mother looked for years through letters
and phone calls, and finally in obituaries in three states.
Her photograph is on page 67 in the Stranahan High yearbook.

2. I have found one letter from my father.
Ireland, 1978. A company trip. It is addressed
to *Babe*:

The food is good.
The room is clean.
Bought a stuffed Dalmatian.
Be home soon.

JUNE

(black ink on graph paper)

Masha, Masha,

        watching me tonight,

I can't sleep,
      my eyes shut tight.

Masha, Masha,
      stay with me
          tonight?

What She Said

And this morning she made me so angry. What was it she said? *You miss your life.* That was it. *You miss your life … of course you do, sweetheart. I'm sorry you're stuck here with me.* Like I am some kind of mope. Like I don't try to be patient and kind. Like I don't try to smile.

The Rules

Don't ask a dying woman
how she is doing.

Don't discuss next year, next
Christmas or curable diseases.

Don't sleep in. Don't mention widowers
who date. Remember,

for someone with a pulmonary illness,
a really good joke can be fatal.

Be careful what books you bring to read.

Two Muses

"If you were really, truly happy, you would never even notice if it was winter or summer. If I was back in Moscow, I wouldn't care what the weather was like." (*Three Sisters*, Anton Chekhov)

Who's ever heard of salting a cantaloupe? My mother is reading *Chatelaine*. She doesn't look up.

I have Chekhov's *Three Sisters* open on my lap. I am lonely today, despite having had good dreams. And the sun is even hotter now.

We will go shopping, for something to do. Attempting small tasks is supposed to help the anxious feeling.

You don't look well, honey, my mother tells me.
Go take a walk outside. Why not
get your hair cut? How about
giving Tammy a call?

I have to separate pages 14 and 15 from a dribble of honey.
There is sweat between my fingers. The kitchen fan
is fumbling above my head. The last time
I read from this copy, I was living
below the Buttes Chaumont
on a tiny side street that has gardens
in front of the houses.

Yesterday we had news from the doctor.
Lung capacity has dropped another couple percent.

I want to do something unwarranted. I want to
smash the bone china in the yard.

I have come to the part when, despite their incessant talk,
(*to Moscow, to Moscow,* they recite)
it becomes clear that Maria, Olga and Irina
are never going to leave
their father's home.

Yalta, 19xx (1)

Chekhov to Olga

Dear Doggie,

Thank you for your sweet letter. I have been in the garden
with the hounds most days. Gorki was here. I'm much better.
They are building a shipyard. Very noisy. And just when I feel
I could write, there is a knock at the door. You would laugh
if you could see me deal with the curious ladies. We eat the biscuits
Masha left for me. You would surely be jealous of their plump cheeks!
By now haven't you found a lover? If you cheat I won't blame you.
I remember Moscow! I've no news from Danchenko, which is odd.

I press your hand in mine, loving, Chekhov.

THE MOSCOW ARRANGEMENT

From time to time, Maria and Olga
shared a flat in Moscow. Olga did her best
to be a good hostess between rehearsals

and parties. Said kind things to everyone
about her sister-in-law. They swore
not to keep secrets. So what

if once in a while Maria didn't tell Olga
about his wheezing, or exactly what
the doctor in Yalta had said.

So what if Olga didn't leave Moscow
to care for her husband when she'd promised.
If she fell down drunk. If she let Maria run back
to be with him again
and again.

YALTA, 19XX (2)

Chekhov to Olga

While you are sipping champagne, I'm counting flies on
the loaf. When you're entertaining dull crowds, I'm here
de-dog-earing hoards of books. *Blue,* you say? Remember
your husband and think of the little half-German we both
want to have, if ever we have cause to be in the
same place (before vermin becomes him). It is so dull
to be alone.

Why is it that I'm here and you stay there?

Yours faithfully, C.

Silent Agreement

My mother and I have a silent agreement:
there is no time for new things. So we relive her favourites.
Singin' in the Rain, The Kingston Trio, Swedish rye bread, the time
my dad had to buy me a bicycle because I wouldn't stop riding
around the Canadian Tire when I was only three.

She doesn't keep much food down, especially in the evenings.
I have to help her in the bathroom. Another secret we keep.
She takes rainy days personally now. She won't say it,
but I know what she is living for, how she would kill
to have my sister's baby in her arms even just once.

Early Afternoon

When my sister comes home for the weekend, I set the two of them up on the back porch with a basket of towels and socks to fold. My mother likes these tasks no matter how long they take to finish. They are happy to sit out there together, taking in the sun. My father joins them for a time. Mother goes on about old church board politics, her grandmother's flower gardens in Sweden; she critiques television commercials from memory. There are a lot of things about this life she would change.

Early afternoon is the best time to be out there. Usually you can see a cardinal or two. Maybe once in a while I wonder if they notice that the iced tea is delivered, that the watermelon comes scooped on a platter, that there is homemade rhubarb jam on the flax toast.

Two Tragedies

There was blood on her dress when she got on the train.
Someone said she turned green before fainting.

It took two guards to lift her body from the platform.
She looked like a dead thing being carried away.

Two doctors came in the night to perform a secret operation.
She said she hadn't even known. Must have been the reason

she fainted in Gorki's play the week before.
Stanislavski was with her in the morning. Maria would fetch her

in a few days to bring her to Chekhov's home.
The problem was the timing. She hadn't been to Yalta

three months earlier. Both doctors said she almost
didn't make it. Maria looked after her.

Chekhov moved around with two sticks.
The problem was the timing. This he had to get out

of his head. He could forgive her anything.
She did get better. No miracle.

The problem was the timing.

SEASONS CHANGE

with the blow of an axe
where we are from. Each day
is hotter than the one before.

I have made us gin and tonics
that we drink in the yard
before the minister comes

for her weekly visit.
My mother wipes sweat from her breast
with an embroidered hanky. She has been

a good Lutheran since she can remember.
There's no Lutheran church here. So,
for the last thirty years she's settled

for United. When she was sixteen,
she spent a summer eating fried chicken,
roasted corn and potatoes with all the good

Lutherans of the Northwest. Her mother
had to send a new set of clothes when the ones
she brought would no longer do up. Otherwise

my mother kept her figure— she'll show you
in photographs. The minister's arrival
is my cue to go back inside

where it's probably even hotter. These talks
are private. And I am learning that it's harder
to not believe in God.

I wonder how Maria managed to lie the way I do.
No, no, Chekhov's well, the goat's milk has worked a treat.
When Chekhov died, Olga had taken him to Germany.

It was a day or two before Maria got word. Olga
gave Chekhov a Lutheran funeral in a little church

near Badenweiler. She would have buried him there
too if weren't for the telegrams:
Bring Chekhov home!

He was returned to Moscow by train, his body
boxed alongside a fellow countryman's.
They rode the whole way in an airtight oyster car.

Quiet Hours

*"I am terribly bored…I get up when it is still dark. Imagine it is dark, the wind
blows and the rain beats on the window."* (From a Letter to an Unknown
Recipient, Anton Chekhov)

What time is it? My mother's voice startles
from behind her book.

What no one ever mentions is how boring it is to be ill.

The days here are measured
in better-than and worse-than yesterdays. Today
will be better. There are birds on the lawn.

I have given her a new, dust-free copy
of "An Anonymous Story." She got annoyed
with the wife in "Lady With a Lapdog"
before getting to the end.

Couldn't you find something a little more uplifting?

We go through the lists:

*Pay CAA membership. Pomegranate juice. You have to manually
turn the coffee pot off, open the dryer door, keep silver in plastic bags,
milk for your father, weeds among the patio stones.*

She has always been good at preparing
for things. I found her starting
to dress at five this morning
when I let the dog out to run.
Forty-five minutes
for her trousers alone.

We go to the shops before lunch
to minimize our chances of seeing
people we might know. Today

we learn that we can move
best with a grocery basket
balanced on her lap, the wheelchair
on loan from Dad's friend, Al.

Get some nice preserves for Leona, she says.

When I come back, she is still
in aisle ten, fruit and veg. She is helping a young boy,
no more than thirteen,
to smell out a good tomato.

My Sister

never climbed out the window in the middle of the night to drink
beer on the hill by the 7-Eleven, never dropped acid

on the football field before a school dance. She got scholarships,
a secure job with a good salary and full benefits; she speaks Spanish

and still holds a high school record for the triple jump. If she'd been
the one to come home, she would have thought of taking our mother

to the States; she would have researched lung transplants. But she can't
know how quickly things are changing. That's what I'll have to

remember later when she doesn't understand. Why I didn't always
mention the regular vomiting, the bruises.

Maria said her brother screamed in the night.

Yalta, 19xx (3)

Chekhov to Olga

If you tell me to believe you, I will. I've no use for rumour
and gossip. I don't go checking after you, and any abuse you
think you're taking is your matter. You can see being in Yalta
has its advantages. Although some distraction would be a welcome
change. You'll be on your feet in no time and running to your
sour husband whose life is a bore. Darling, you know you have
great power over this mind that awaits you.

I take your hand in mine. Anton.

The Remnants

They say Bunin loved her,
pressed his body up to hers, pushed notes
under her door when he came to stay.

As best she could, Maria kept her passions
to herself. Privately preferred laudanum
to sex. It is there in the photographs,
the young girl with bullets for eyes. Her students
said there was no one better. They
folded petals into their work.

But none of this is left
in her letters.

My Father

I keep a pen and paper to scrawl things down.

Over the years my father has found my notes
around the house, but never asked me about them.

It's quite a book you must be writing, he says today out of the blue.

We go through the house searching
for mould, dust, poison. But
the doctor says, *Sometimes illness is just
one of those things.* He doesn't realize

what a shrug of the shoulders
means. How my father will blame
himself if there isn't some other answer.

How he will go over everything. Eventually
he will tell two friends. They will be out eating
doughnuts after a round of golf.

On a September night in 1951, Olga Knipper stayed up
half the night going over old lines, the parts Chekhov
wrote for her, as though hearing them for the first time.

She had been so young. How could she
have understood what was really being said?
Her secretary, who slept in the next room,

noted it was as if she were speaking
to old friends. Olga never quit the theatre
to be with Chekhov. Her Moscow apartment

was on the seventh floor, without a lift. Each
time they parted, he left in a worsened condition.

If she could only play Madame Ranevskaya
in *The Cherry Orchard* now.

My father tells his friends about my notes,
and they nod in some kind of understanding.
But when they go home to their respective wives,
they don't mention the doughnuts, or
the tremble in his voice, or that he got lost
driving them home.

CHEKHOV'S BISHOP DREAMS

"... everything around was young and warm and near, everything—the trees and the sky and even the moon—and one longed to feel that it would always be so."
("The Bishop," Anton Chekhov)

of eating cakes, and telling dirty jokes
and drinking whiskey
until the wee hours
in the parlour. Pretty girls
in pretty dresses, their cheeks
the colour of wine. And
rest without fear,
sleep before death.
To be anonymous
again, but not
forgotten.

Unsent Letter 3

To:
9 Cité Jandelle
Paris, 75019

Dearest J.,

*The daffodils are always the first to be supplanted by summer. But what is taking
over the gardens this year? If I were in Paris, I'd still be running in the Buttes
Chaumont each morning. I'd be watching the Vietnamese weddings by the
pond.*

*You will go to the allotment in Montreuil where small boys play football against
the painted garage doors. S. will bring wine and a salad: olives, fennel
and sliced orange.*

*At the end of the dirt patch where tomatoes are growing, patio stones make
a terrace for the lawn chairs you'll bring. You can imagine that the sea is there in
the distance. I was always in charge of getting the fire going. Do you remember?*

What was it you always said? C'est la grande vie quand les groseilles
poussent bien. *They're sown on the east side of the plot. No neighbours again
this year.*

The last time we were there, you were about to tell me a story.

Yalta, 19xx (4)

Chekhov to Olga

Tolstoy was here. Thinks I should
reconsider my religion.

JULY

(blue ink on Benadryl card)

Dearest Masha,

Things are changing again.

We have propped up the head of the bed to keep her from choking while she sleeps. My father decided on stacked coffee tins.

We are using the big ones—Maxwell House.

P.S. How did you stay so good? Do you remember how good you were?

"Everywhere is a desert to the lonely man." (ring inscription, Pavel Chekhov)

Yalta, 19xx (5)

Chekhov to Olga

We spend so little time together, I don't even know
if you talk to yourself.

It's so dry here.

All my love,
Anton.

Water Baby

This morning we bought an air conditioner. My father will install it tonight, once it cools down. I helped my mother to get into the pool today. She loves to float on the foam raft with her head back, semi-submerged. She can move her legs freely in the water. She doesn't seem to get out of breath. She watches the clouds pass overhead. I wonder what they make her think about.

My Sister

sits with my mother on the porch, husking corn on the cob for our dinner. She protects her belly with a softly cupped hand and smiles. Their shoulders go up and down at something my mother has said. I watch them through the kitchen window. She will go home in the morning. Mother has said she is feeling much better and should be able to visit soon. There is a bakery where the three of us can have lunch.

They let the silky yellow strands of husk blow off the table, miss the garbage bag I set up for just this reason. The strands catch wind and take off across the grass, eventually sinking into the clear waters of the swimming pool. They dance there like reeds in the shallows of a small ocean.

BADENWEILER, GERMANY

When Chekhov and Olga arrived in Badenweiler,
he spent his days jotting notes to loved ones,
dreaming of Italian lakes, nights in Trieste
and delicate almond biscuits— the powdered kind
that dissolve into nothing
on the tongue.

Dearest Masha,
(He sat at his desk, a glass of seltzer water next to his pot of ink.)

I am already better. Tell everyone. Health is coming back to me.
(Even his fingers were shrinking.)

P.S. Olga is going to a dentist. I don't notice now, as I go about, that I am ill.

Hotel Sommer, Badenweiler

(Several Days Later)
Chekhov to Olga

Darling Doggie,

My sweet love, as I write, you are laughing in the next room,
entertaining the young brothers this evening. How we—you—
found two Russian Rabenecks(!), to be sure, in Badenweiler, I'll never
know. Today when you went to Freiburg, I walked the garden, almost
got caught in a squabble with two drunk Germans. Leo came to my
rescue. We had a chat about fishing. I dream of it, and of you—seeing
you arrive by train, your hat blowing. There's nothing we can do
now. I feel it coming. Be well. Don't mourn. Remember this.

I take your hand in mine.

Hotel Sommer

(Still in Badenweiler)

The room is hot. Outside the sun is at its height. Clothes are strewn over the two chairs on the left-hand side of the bed. A broad-rimmed woman's hat is hanging on a hook. A game of solitaire is set out on the little writing desk. There is a painting of a willow tree on the plastered wall.

Unsent Letter 4

To:
9 Cité Jandelle
Paris, 75019

Dearest J.,

How are you? How is the city?

I have been painting you a portrait of A.C. from a photograph I keep.
It's the one where he's wearing a checkered tie.

It's his eyes that I can't get right.

THE DAY THEY COME

Leona, the neighbour, is the first to meet the triple-response team
when they arrive on our lawn. My mother's stats dropped during a routine

checkup first thing in the morning. They had to unplug the oxygen machine
to get her on the stretcher and plug her into a more reliable heart. There is no

space for me in the small room. So many hands, so many shoulders. Then,
everything goes into slow motion. A voice asks if I've packed a bag,

the pill list, what's she eaten, how long has she been like this? As he slips
a tube up her shirt, one of the workers recognizes my mother as his former

keyboarding teacher from 1999. He tells me this smiling, his white teeth
beaming against the black-brown of his summer tan.

AUGUST

(pencil on white notepaper)

Masha,

I've been making lists

of all the ways

I don't want

to die.

AT NOON BY THE FIFTH FLOOR WINDOW

I tell you this story
as you fall in and out of sleep
in your hospital bed.

*The dry wind howled as the train left the station. Maria Chekhova was taking
the arduous three-week journey from Yalta to Moscow by herself. The stifling air
in the carriage reeked of cigarette smoke. The men and women on the train were
brown with sun and dust. It was the summer of 1921.*

We have come to the end
of a long summer. Last
night it rained for the
first time in weeks.

*She was going to secure some of his papers that had long been left in the city.
When they arrived in Simferopol, she was forced into another carriage. A
luggage carrier full of even more peasants than the last. Standing room only.*

Your body is working
hard to keep up
with the machines
that blink all day and all
night like a train
approaching from
a distance.

"Bourgeois! Get her off this train," the peasants yelled when they saw how Maria was dressed, the leather case she held. She tried to make herself as small as possible so that the yelling would stop. She tried to hide her face in the frenzied crowd.

I offer you water.
You take
very little.

A woman next to Maria had a little boy at her side. The boy was reading one of Chekhov's stories, "Van'ka." "Do you know who that is?" Maria asked, pointing to the spine. "Anton Chekhov," said the boy. "Well, that's my brother," the old woman said and smiled.

Your eyes open again.
This is your kind of story.

When the boy's mother realized it was true, she gave Maria food and water and stayed with her until it was time to go off in separate directions.

I take your hand in mine.
When I arrived this morning,
you were scared. You
wrote on a pad of white paper
that you thought they might
intubate tonight. Yesterday
I promised I wouldn't let them; now
we both know the impossibility of things.

The little boy waved until Maria was completely out of sight, and when he could no longer see her, he told his mother that he would pray for her safe journey home.

I tell you this story because
I started praying last night.
Nothing too sophisticated,
just what you showed me
a long time ago.

JACKSONVILLE

*"There is neither morality nor logic in my being a doctor and your being a ...
patient, there is nothing but idle chance."* ("Ward No.6," Anton Chekhov)

The photograph is dated
1963, *Jacksonville* scribbled across
the back. You are posed
by the pier, wearing stilettos
like you often did in those days, your blouse open
just so—as a child
I dreamt about your past life, used to practise posing
like you, draped in one of Dad's shirts, arms akimbo,
a belt wrapped tight around my little frame,
the bottoms of my heels pressed
against the arches of your shoes.

Tonight your heart leaps heavily against that
beautiful freckled chest. *A summer spent*
by the pool, it says.
I am growing tired, it says.
I lick my thumb and wipe
a smudge off your cheek. I am holding
a straw to your mouth when
the doctor comes in. He is young. He is handsome.
He flirts with you but he doesn't know
how beautiful you are behind that plastic mask. He has never
heard you say *Good morning* or tasted wild blueberry cake
fresh from your oven.

I want to show him the Jacksonville
shot to see if your beauty can inspire a miracle.
I want to shake him into God. I want
to smell you once more, the backs
of my white thighs stuck to your bare
knees while you talk on the telephone.
I want you to be here
in the morning.

Code Blue

We went out for dinner on the lakefront,
to that little restaurant that's changed hands
so many times. We ate

slowly and talked about nothing,
ordered three Cokes with our food. After
dinner we walked by the oil drums

and picked up lucky stones from the gritty sand.
We launched thin ones out into the waves while
the sun grew giant before us. We did not
hurry about a thing.

Maybe one of us knew it would happen that night
and that was why we went back long after
visiting hours. But when we got there,
a code blue meant that we had to wait.

It took us a few moments to realize
the perfect young doctors racing past
us were headed for your room.

If only we'd been braver, we'd have
burst through the doors ourselves, forced our way
like good villains. When you could still speak,

the last thing you were able to ask me
was where all of your worry would go.

My Sister

pretended I was hers when they first brought me home. They made her
wear a mask because of her cold, but there she is in the photograph,

holding me. Each night she got out of bed to watch me, pretending
she could read my dreams. I spied on her for one whole summer.

She drank cases of Doctor Pepper, read the Dollanganger series and swore
she had ESP. That was the summer we both believed we could do anything.

The Minister's Visit

At midnight, when the mosquitoes have finally grown tired,
Leona is awake to watch the exodus.
Her porch light still on after they've fled.

This is how she sees when the minister arrives.
He crosses her lawn on the way to our door.

Even though she has been waiting all summer for this,
his arrival causes her heart to flutter,
Oh, God no, oh God no,
the voice inside her says.

Her worn-out body
makes it to the couch just before
her legs collapse. She rests there, returning
to the position that she has already spent
most of the night in, and so many nights in,

next to her T.V. remote, next to her half-finished pile
of Cheetos delicately placed on a patterned paper towel.

Leona makes a shopping list of supplies
for a quiche to bring over to the house.
She writes a card that she keeps
for just such an occasion.

When she is finished, she cries
for everything bad that has ever been.
Not because this loss
is so great, but because loss
is a reminder of other losses.

Her little spaniel presses his claws
into her thick thighs and licks the orange powder
from her fingers. He sniffs
the corners of her eyes tenderly,
and she even thinks she hears him whisper,
I am here, Leona.

Before going to bed, she pulls
the heavy curtains so that no light can get in.
There will be so much more
to do in the morning.

DEAREST MARIA,

I know where the worry goes. I know where
the worry goes. I know where the worry goes.
I know where the worry goes. I know where
the worry goes. I know where the worry goes.
I know where the worry goes. I know where
the worry goes. I know where the worry goes.
I know where the worry goes. I know where
the worry goes. I know where the worry goes.
I know where the worry goes. I know where
the worry goes. I know where the worry goes.
I know where the worry goes. I know where
the worry goes.

SEPTEMBER

(pencil on brown paper bag)

Oh, Masha,

what have I done?

I should have told her everything.

A Photograph before Death

Near the end of the first act
of *Three Sisters*, Fedotik
takes a photograph of all the dinner guests
who've shown up at Irina's birthday party. It's Chekhov's way
of preparing us—someone is about to die.

In this last photograph of you,
taken only a week or so before your funeral, your shoulders
are tanned from the afternoon sun. You protested
every request for a photograph I made all summer, every
time I asked you to smile. But in this last image
you look happy.

I didn't take this photograph. It's you and dad
in the swimming pool, his arm around you.
Your oxygen hose hovers over the water, it traipses
out of view across the patio stones and
makes a mad dash into the distance.

Like a rascal child, it crushes
some carefully planted agapanthuses.

Belaya Dacha, 19xx and 19xx

Every time the uniformed men
arrived at the white house in Yalta,
stomped their boots on the porch
overlooking the flowering fig trees and quince,
Maria was always already hungry.

Her brother was now long gone. She'd hired a girl
for support in the raids. And there was even less
food to go around, with the incessant mewing
of cats at the door.

Maria gave the intruders rules upon entry.
Mostly they did as they were told.

They washed their hands after using the toilet,
stubbed out their cigarettes in broken clay pots, picked the horse shit
from their boots before coming inside. She felt lucky. Everybody had heard
about Dostoyevsky's house.

The looting would go on for hours. They often
took more than her food. Shots in the night broke windows
and whispered a kind of violence. But no one, not the bandits
nor the anti-Bolsheviks nor the Whites
would go into his room.

When it happened again with the Germans,
she had a few days to prepare the house.
She hung Goethe where Gorki had been.
Set out photos of the dachshunds and
German translations of her brother's work.

What I know of war is a certain kind of prison.
Maria couldn't get the words out of her head.
I too am like a prisoner.
But what is this prisoner like?

My Father's House

He doesn't erase her handwriting
on the kitchen whiteboard
or throw anything out
from the fridge. Her glasses sit
unfolded on the dresser.

THE NIGHT BEFORE SHE DIED

Maria dreamed of the yard in Yalta.
All of the fruit trees were crying
and she didn't know why. The dogs were there.
Olga too, just back from America, eating a giant
pumpkin pie in the shade. Maria sat down
in the middle of the lawn and began to laugh.
She laughed so hard her stomach cramped and
then her feet began to rise involuntarily.
The movement continued to her knees and hips,
and before she knew it, she was floating upside down,
her dress billowing in the warm breeze,
and still she was laughing, utterly and
uncontrollably now. The trees stopped crying
to look at her, and all at once they began laughing too.

The Tenant of Regret

If Olga had lived with him
in the white house by the sea,
he never would have had time to write.
At least, that was what he said. And yet
later on it was as if the years had passed before him,
and all of a sudden he missed the time they'd never had.

Sometimes, as he became more confined to his bed
under the bow window, he would think she was there
beside him. He would fight her for the pillows and sheets.
Other times he would call out her name.

When the telephone rings, I think
for a moment it will be my mother.
I can see her in the lamplight
of her living room, twisting the phone cord
around her left hand, rocking
in the sturdy brown chair.

In a residential neighbourhood not so far from the Moscow Arts Theatre, Olga Knipper-Chekhova, Russia's most enduring actress, in her ninety-first year sat waiting in a creaking captain's chair for her girl to return. The girl was about to do her feet. Her leg lay propped on a tatty stool. She held the newspaper from the previous day. She needed morning light, and the paper never arrived until afternoon. *I've never missed a cue in my life*, she called, in the direction of the kitchen sink, where a bucket was filling with hot water. The girl manipulated the faucets with a certain expertise. Outside, the air was cool and wet. The thaw was in its early stages and young people were gathering on the sidewalks once more. *Ask Stanislavski!* she carried on. Of course, the girl—only twenty-three—was only half-paying attention, the task at hand being quite enough. And the old actress was always so pleased when the water temperature was just right for her feet. The girl didn't know Stanislavski anyway, nor could she have asked him if she did. Stanislavski was dead. Dead. Meierhold, Nemirovich, Kachalov, Lilina, Vishnevski. Long dead. The actress scratched a tiny patch of dry skin below her right knee. On her foot, the bunion that would soon be filed down, turned to dust, ready for another to take its place.

That Old Season

I wonder what will happen to things like Christmas. To that summer
when I was eleven and we rented a cottage on the lake in Muskoka. I
will go on but I will not be ready for the dreams. The dreams that say
you are still alive and dying, dying and still alive. The dreams where I
forget about you in rooms I have also forgotten. Dreams where, even
though I try to hold you, you jump from Ferris wheels and I see your
swollen body hit the ground. Yes, I will go on. Yes, I will get better
and throw myself into things. I will, on occasion, take pills to breathe.
I will still want to break plates when you have been dead long enough
to call it the past. That old season. Like when the light, inside and out,
was different for a while. I write down most things in a kind of letter:
this is what we did while you were gone.

Knipper's Death

She'd prepared certain things,
like fresh azaleas, clean underclothes,
placed her favourite photographs in view.

She didn't drink champagne,
didn't special order a funeral shroud.
On the mantelpiece, a card inscribed
Last card from Masha, to help her biographers
through the lot.

When it came out in the papers, most of Russia
stopped drinking its tea
for a moment.

They thought she had gone
many years before.

AFTER

ARCHIVE

On the blank blank he blank.

How Tolstoy came to see him.

He sent Olga 400 kisses, August 13, 1900.

He kept *Hamlet* next to his bed.

He never mentions tuberculosis (except in the early play, *Ivanov*, although his characters are virtually always sick).

There are three Chekhov House Museums. One holds the originals, while the other two hold duplicates of his possessions.

Facsimiles of a good life, including a replica of a bench that Gorki sat on, replica pillows on his beds, and replica shaving kits.

Levitan was his very dear friend.

The first time he got sick was en route to his grandfather's. The second time was going to the island (Sakhalin) in the middle of Siberia with wet boots.

*

We keep your dresses hung neatly in the cupboard, under the linen tablecloths and the silver punch bowl.

Albuquerque, New Mexico

Mother and Two Unidentified Others, 19xx

You are straddling a stranger in the photograph. I can see the shape of his large shoulders, the breadth of his chest, as he lies on the bed beneath you.

And there is a girl with you in the room. She is the one who has captured you both in the shot. Her camera and reflection in the mirror. It wasn't like you to get caught.

It's strange I care so much about who they are or whether or not you loved him, or if he was good to you, your twenty-something self. This photograph doesn't even belong to me. I just happened to find it among your other private things.

Margaree, Nova Scotia

I have taken you back to the ocean of your reveries, your past life. I
have brought you east and I have planted you here so that the sunshine
can wake you. You will stay with me until I catch up to you in years, no
matter how long it takes. We are only a kilometer from the ocean. The
river is close enough to sound like a bath running. I remember how you
loved hot baths even in the summertime, especially in the summertime.
You would let me open the door and talk to you. Sitting cross-legged on
the shag carpet where the hall and cold tiles met, I asked if God was a real
man. *He was,* you told me. *Without question.*

A Visit to the National Portrait Gallery, London

Last Portrait of Mother by Daphne Todd

Almost a landscape painting—
the body on the pillows,
the light that ripples
over bone. The sound
of her last breath. The one
everyone talks about. The one that would
leave the mouth agape
for eternity.

Hers is a Levitan portrait, by her daughter.
The grain-coloured flesh of a mother
three days gone. She is painted
with her hospital bracelet
still on.

A woman stands beside me,
holding a child's wrist in her hand.
I recognize the child's glance
looking up at her.

I had a letter from Paris today. J. is travelling
with her mother to Egypt after all.

Ever been to the southwest of England? I ask. You are a friend I haven't known since high school, but we've been meeting up regularly since I've been home. While I am staying with my dad, we go out in the evenings to do yoga and eat fast food. You are all that I know here anymore. *No,* you say, and shake your head. Two mobile phones strapped to your waist belt for the booze-delivery business you run. Your burger dripping onto the paper wrap you have neatly unfolded across your lap. The evening is humid for October and we are sitting in your new Ford.

I saw a rainbow once when I was a child, in Bristol on the Gloucester Road. It looked like it was coming out of the spire at St. Anne's. It was so beautiful that we felt sorry for the people walking in the wrong direction who couldn't see it. We wanted to shout *rainbow* the way you would shout *whale* on a tourist boat, half-knowing that by the time anyone heard us it would have disappeared.

It's the way it rains there, I say after a moment. At first it barely makes you wet. Then all at once it quickens into a flood of bucketing showers. It belts down so hard the drops bounce back up and explode. *It must be something to be a fish in the river there,* you say. When the rain stops, it's like it never happened and everyone goes on their way.

That's how the tears come now. They surprise me and they're gone.

Closed Doors

I'll never know how my parents loved,
their bedroom door closed tight,
the sturdy furniture too big
for a room its size.

Or why we followed my father's car
in our New Yorker that time we saw him
on a street that wasn't his usual way home.
We didn't honk, or mention it later.

Were there certain perfumes he liked
more than others? Did he ever notice?
I wonder now if he sometimes takes the bottles
off the dresser, holds them

to his nose for a moment
while my sister, on the other side
of the door, picks up
the mess he needs to make.

There are things I hope
about my mother. I hope she felt
love each time they promised one another
everything would be alright.

UNSENT LETTER 5

To:
9 Cité Jandelle
Paris, 75019

It's strange who you tell and don't tell about death.

For a while it made me stronger. I could walk confidently into any situation feeling I had sufficiently suffered.

We are lucky, my sister says, to have known the unconditional kind of love.

The Hospital Notes

They moved me into here. They are keeping a better eye on me. I can't get up. The nurse last night was really good.

Hi, kiddo. Dorothy was here. Nice. What are you doing? Don't worry. Promise not to worry. Promise. I love you.

I've been awake since six! You should come first thing in the morning! Did you get doggy diapers? Anybody call? Don't tell them I'm here. Only P. and B. Where's your father?

I ate half my pizza. Wasn't bad. Feel a bit better today. I like your shoes. You should keep your hairbrush in your purse. You can get a chair if you want. Anybody call?

You sure gave me some hard times, kiddo. Of course I do. My baby. I am so lucky to have such wonderful girls. Thanks for coming home. I don't know what I would have done without you.

P.S. I'd like you to send flowers to the nurse from the first night. She was really good.

Tonight they want to put tubes down my throat. Don't leave me. That damn doctor.

It's everything I'm going to miss.

A Passage

Even in the silent movie there are words we understand. Words like *breathe* and *stop* and *I know you are not coming back.*

I trickle water on the violets anyway,

      smash the china plate like your best friend's mother did when you were eight, over for dinner, and not supposed to see. The lamb-shank juice like blood on the flocked wallpaper.

      I can still see you and sense you.

      A month before his death, Anton Chekhov scribbled a note to Masha, *Live happily and don't be down.*

It is a soft passage into the night.

A Dream

I imagine this boy,
a small boy. Someone to have driven toy cars with,
built complicated forts with, deep
in the woods. I see him
healthy.

My mother is there. She is rosy-cheeked
and no taller than the seat of a chair.
She keeps her distance, watches me and the boy play.
Each time I almost get close to her, she moves on,
disappears.

Since no one else is around,
I concentrate on the boy.
We throw marbles in the sand
out of purple and gold bags;
grow old and tired enough
to fall asleep.

I've heard a lot of people
have this dream.

NOTES ON THE TEXT

p. 19. "Bromide" was the name of Chekhov's dachshund.

p. 21. In "Unsent Letter 1," the last stanza is an adaptation of the final passage in Chekhov's "The Beauties."

p. 28. Chekhov was himself famous among his friends for spying and eavesdropping. (See Michael Finke's *Seeing Chekhov,* Cornell University Press, 2005.)

p. 43. Olga Knipper was playing Arkadina in *The Seagull* when she met Chekhov.

p. 54, 56, 65, 71, 76, 80. The poems entitled "Yalta, 19xx" are based on the collected letters of Anton Chekhov and Olga Knipper, translated and edited by Jean Benedetti, but do not attempt to replicate any one letter, nor do they quote directly from them.

p. 59. In 1902 Olga Knipper suffered a miscarriage. Donald Rayfield, among others, speculates that her pregnancy was the result of an affair. This affair has never been proven, and many Russian scholars reject this idea altogether. "Two Tragedies" is also the title of one of Chekhov's short stories.

p. 66. In fact, the majority of Maria's letters do not remain.

p. 70. The final two stanzas in this poem borrow indirectly from Chekhov's "The Gooseberries."

p. 79. In this poem I have loosely quoted letters sent by Chekhov to Maria from Badenweiler in June of 1904, translated by Constance Garnett in *Letters of Anton Chekhov* (The Project Gutenberg Ebook, 2004).

p. 88. The italicized sections are based on an anecdote in Harvey Pitcher's *Chekhov's Leading Lady* (John Murray, 1979), but the story has been put into my own words.

p. 103. I am indebted to W.D. Wetherell for the way he imagined Maria's response to the German invasion of the house in *Chekhov's Sister* (Little, Brown and Company, 1990).

A NOTE ON CHEKHOV

Anton Chekhov was born on January 29, 1860, in Taganrog, Russia. The third of six surviving children, he studied in Moscow to be a physician but ended up falling in love with writing, eventually becoming the prolific author of short stories, short novels and five major plays (*Ivanov, The Seagull, Uncle Vanya, Three Sisters* and *The Cherry Orchard*). Throughout his lifetime he was considered one of the greatest short-story writers of all time, a consensus that endures to this day. Known for both his humility and generosity, he set up free medical clinics for peasants wherever he lived.

Chekhov spent the majority of his life as a tubercular, although he rarely admitted to being ill. In 1890 he went to Sakhalin, in Siberia, to interview inmates at the penal colony and study the region. In 1901 he married the actress (and lead in most of his plays) Olga Knipper in a secret ceremony. The two met during a rehearsal for *The Seagull*. His sister, Maria Chekhova, became his primary caregiver when he moved to Yalta for better air. Their mother, Evgenia, also lived there with them. Knipper remained in Moscow to work, and occasionally Maria would live there with her.

Chekhov died in 1904 in Badenweiler, Germany, having gone with Knipper to the Black Forest town for its good air quality. Chekhov continued to deny his condition until the last moments when, a glass of champagne in hand, he declared *Ich Sterbe*— *I am dying*. Maria Chekhova remained in his home in Yalta and kept it as a Chekhov house museum until her own death. Knipper remained in Moscow, and toured with the Moscow Arts Theatre. Both Knipper and Maria lived through Stalin's regime. Olga Knipper continued to write letters to her husband long after he died.

ACKNOWLEDGEMENTS

My deepest thanks to Stephanie Bolster, Barry Dempster, Jan
Zwicky, John Barton, Carolyn Forché, Nick Thran, Kitty Lewis,
Cheryl Dipede, Sue Sinclair and everyone at Brick Books for their
dedication to this work. Thank you to Mary di Michele, Andre
Furlani and Mikhail Iossel for their contributions. I would like
extend many thanks to the Nova Scotia Department of Tourism,
Culture and Heritage for their financial support. Tremendous
gratitude to the Ladies' Auxiliary (C. Cooper, S. Faber, M.K. Carr,
R. Silver Slayter, and J. Parr) for early readings of these poems.

I would like to acknowledge the gracious support, both past
and present, of R. Heikkila, M. Norman, K. Armstrong, L.
Monteith, the Martyn family, the Clark family, A. Wallington, C.
Polzot, V. Mersereau, A. Clark, J. Skibsrud, D. Pearn, J. Laurent,
T. Southcott, S. and R. Martyn.

Thank you to Matthew Parsons, whose love, patience and faith in me
and my project has been beyond measure. Thank you to my loving
family.

This is for M. Parsons, A. Parsons, G. Vear, J. Skibsrud, A.
Wallington, G. Vazquez, C. Robertson, L. Whitton, N. Taylor,
S. Swaffield, S. Faber, M. Paddon, L. Paddon, W. West, S. Bergeron,
J. Fraser, D. Paddon, P. Paddon, B. Richards, S. Will, K. Dickens, J.
West, A. Thomson, N. Jones, H. Walling, S. Macaskill, G. Anderson's
family, N. Anderson's family, R. Anderson's family, the Hepburn
family, the Watson family, the Andrews family, and everyone who
lost a parent far too soon.

I am indebted to the work on Chekhov by Donald Rayfield, Ronald Hingley, Harvey Pitcher, Michael Finke, Jean Benedetti and, of course, to Anton Chekhov.

My gratitude goes out to the following magazines and publications for accepting some of the poems in this collection for publication:

Geist Magazine, The Antigonish Review, CV2, Eleven Eleven, Sifted, Desperately Seeking Susans and *Arc Poetry Magazine.*

Susan Paddon's poetry has appeared in *The Antigonish Review, Arc Poetry Magazine, Desperately Seeking Susans, Eleven Eleven, Sifted, CV2* and *Geist Magazine,* among others. After attending McGill University, she moved to London, England, for several years before moving to Paris, France, where she met her husband. She writes poetry, short fiction and screenplays, and is currently working on a novel. She now lives with her husband in Margaree, Cape Breton.